"Rather than words comes the thought of high windows:
The sun-comprehending glass,
And beyond it, the deep blue air, that shows
Nothing, and is nowhere, and is endless."

~ Philip Larkin

Also by Kieran Egan

Amplified Silence – Silver Bow Publishing, 2021

Tenure. Edmonton: NeWest Press, 2021.

Among the branches (Alfred Gustav Press) 2019

Learning in depth: A simple innovation that can transform schooling. Chicago: University of Chicago Press, 2011.

The future of education: Reimagining our schools from the ground up. New Haven: Yale University Press, 2008.

Building my Zen garden. Boston: Houghton Mifflin, 2000.

The Educated mind: How cognitive tools shape our understanding. Chicago: University of Chicago Press, 1997.

Teaching as story telling. Chicago: University of Chicago Press, 1989.

More books by Kieran Egan at:
https://www.thriftbooks.com/a/kieran-egan/308780/

Seven Oaks Ago

by

Kieran Egan

720 – Sixth Street, Box # 5
New Westminster, BC
CANADA V3C 3C5

Title: Seven Oaks Ago
Author: Kieran Egan
Layout and Design: Candice James
Editor: Candice James

www.silverbowpublishing.com
© Silver Bow Publishing
info@silverbowpublishing.com

isbn: 9781774031919 book
isbn: 9781774031926 e book

Library and Archives Canada Cataloguing in Publication

Title: Seven oaks ago / by Kieran Egan.
Names: Egan, Kieran, author.
Description: Poems.
Identifiers: Canadiana (print) 20210376058 | Canadiana (ebook) 20210376066 | ISBN 9781774031919
   (softcover) | ISBN 9781774031926 (EPUB)
Classification: LCC PS8609.G36 S48 2022 | DDC C811/.6—dc23

5

To my beloved Michael, Catherine, and David

Praise for "Seven Oaks Ago"

"This is poetry that is not afraid to tackle big questions about how we live and why we live. We follow a man through his life from youth 'til old age; a man who grapples with the big ideas of our time, the rapid and bewildering changes he has observed and reflects on his role within the natural world. This is a collection that dissects tyranny and dictatorship, the minds of great thinkers and powerful monsters, yet extols the true beauty of trees in sunlight, the way the moon rises to reveal the silhouettes of a dog and a fisherman, and the way trees project against an evening light as seen from the window of a country bus"   **~ Alan Hill, author of "In the Blood"**

Kieran Egan is an explorer of the past, present and future. He interrogates interpreted and remembered pasts, a frightening present, and a number of possible futures. He examines the mundane existence we all forget and countless childhood memories. By the end of the work, all these pasts, presents and futures, all the hopes, dreams, fears and recollections Egan holds up to the light congeal into a wonderful and terrifying reality the reader has to step into. This work is a cartography of a surreal existence that lies just beyond our fingertips if only we have the courage to see it and remember it. **~ Angelo Letizia, assistant professor Notre Dame University, Maryland USA and author of "*The Starry Devil*" and *"Pilgrims of Infinity".***

The poems in Kieran Egan's *Seven Oaks Ago* deftly transport us to a multi-faceted, lyrical realm where the past and present coexist. "Why would the branches whisper to me of Caesar?" Ancient battles, real and conceived events from history and myth are interwoven with vivid snapshots of the poet's childhood where he grapples with moral principles to a philosophical ease in adulthood examining life's complexities. Careful observation and deep appreciation of the natural world add spiritual nourishment to his later years. In-depth knowledge of diverse topics, a playful imagination and linguistic finesse create a breathtaking voyage that is immensely satisfying. ~ **Doris Fiszer author of "*Locked in Different Alphabets" shortlisted for the Archibald Lampman Award 2021.***

Kieran Egan's second collection of poems, **Seven Oaks Ago**, takes the reader on a narrative journey where lines blur between history, myth, fact and fiction. Thoughtful and taut these poems tell stories from a myriad of eras and times, from Greek Mythology to Modern times. With precision and clarity Egan speaks to the reader of regimes and wars, memories and moments in time that are captured with tender nostalgia while history looms above. There is much to ruminate in this fine collection that will invite readers to return to its pages again and again. **~ Susan J. Atkinson, author of *"The Marta Poems"*.**

Acknowledgements:

I am grateful for the reading and comments on all or some of these poems by Susanna Egan, Ann Pearson, Christopher Levenson, Allan Briesmaster, members of the delightful A-Drift Writers' Collective (Leanne Boschman, Adrienne Drobnies, Bill Ellis, Tom Gorman, Ken Klonsky, Christopher Levenson, Robin Pacific, Nilofar Shidmehr, and Malcolm van Delst). I was a beneficiary of the poetry class taught by Evelyn Lau and Fiona Lam at the Simon Fraser University downtown campus, in which drafts of some of these poems were written and critiqued.

Some of these poems have appeared in the Canadian magazines *Event, Canadian Literature, The New Quarterly, Quills, Dalhousie Review, Grain, Qwerty, Antigonish Review, Vallum, Canadian Quarterly, Ekphrastic Review, Spadina Literary Review, Pace, Prairie Fire*, and in the anthology *Old Bones and Battered Bookends* (Repartee Press, Canada), and in the UK in *High Window, Orbis, Envoi, Acumen, HQ Poetry Magazine, Interpreter's House, Dream Catcher, Dawntreader, Sarasvati, Dissonance and The Poetry Shed*. I am grateful to their editors for permission to reprint them here.

CONTENTS

And Battles Long Ago

Myth and History

A Cloistered Virtue

Life and Loves

Trees, Birds, Fish, and Things

11

And Battles Long Ago

12

Iron Crosses in Australia

I deal with miners, now that Dad's retired:
we sell safety gear, helmets, masks, and such.
"If you go down — We'll get you out!" we claim.
Diamonds, and nickel, iron, zinc, and lead
bring me on this trip into the Kimberley.

After a mine tour, my demos and address,
the owner invited me to dinner.
Before the meal our hosts' four grandchildren
played a Mozart string quartet,
with expert skill, as far as I could tell.
We stood to clap the smiling players,
and only then I saw above the fire,
in pride of place, a painting of our host's
handsome father, in crisp new uniform,
an iron cross assertive at his throat,
another on his field-grey jacket pocket,
an eagle's talons round a swastika.
Red collar tabs with oak leaves,
and red-rimmed shoulder boards, with three gold pips.
It shocked me, but I kept my face in check.

He was a *Gruppenführer*, said my host,
whose bones lie somewhere in the grassy fields
near the family's lost estate. He died
slowing the unstoppable Red Army
while the population, and his family,
ran in mad panic west from Königsberg.

I lay in bed above that room and portrait.
Unfamiliar sounds; cane toads, they'd told me,
and frogs, and maybe a few bandicoot.
Mine safety rules, Mozart, iron crosses,
my host's blue eyes, the smiling blond quartet.
A busy day, a rich contract secured.
Outside, bats cleared the air of insects.

The Last Siren

We kids were playing marbles in the street
one day when all our parents opened doors
and came along the short paths to their gates,
grandparents too, and then stood silently.
Some smiled shyly at their neighbours, but most
looked down, or at the sky, as though in church
attending some solemn ceremony.
Our game stopped as we gawped at the odd sight
of adults quietly just standing there.

The screaming siren shocked our eyes alert;
that iron-shrill commanding urgent whine,
a surging howl, drooping to surge again,
like mad banshees invading English towns.
And then the steady dying all-clear sound:
exactly one year since the end of war.

The men and women, drably clothed, heads down,
their thoughts and feelings hutched into themselves,
retreated to their houses and their lives.
They'd said, of course, at one time or another,
'Thank God it's over', looking at their kids.
But closing doors, how many sensed
their richest years were all behind them now;
the danger, guns and deserts, foreign cities,
intense new friends, the bombs, and reckless love:
emotions they can't recapture or forget —
that final dying siren wailed regret.

Among Stalin's Legacies

"You are — forgive me, sir — an older man,
and you do not, thanks god, look unhappy."
Our Russian guide explains why street merchants
in the Arbat address me in English
though I dress like other idling shoppers.
I look around the train for older men:
thin faces, red-rimmed eyes, or slabs that sag,
undone by vodka and deprivation.
They catch my eye and wish to do me ill.

They have been too long in clanking trains,
each station less glorious than the one from which they started.
The engine slows into a barren field
where the metal wheels screech to a halt.
Onto ice-rimmed clumps of grass, they achingly climb down.
The train sighs into silence where the rails end.
Off to the left, lights through distant trees, and laughter.
Why should not old men wish ill?

Inheritances

The regime was brutal, inept, and, towards the end,
reviled even by its own class-allies.
We were poor but educated, so connoisseurs of injustice.
We had two maps of the city on the wall:
today's with black and red lines, circles, arrows;
tomorrow's pristine, waiting on today's events.

Our wiliest and toughest fighters,
expensively dressed in bourgeois clothes,
mingled with our heroic group
of pregnant women, whom police and soldiers
were reluctant to attack.
Each day, more of their forces deserted.
Their leaders were bewildered by our tactics,
for which they seemed unprepared,
slowed down, no doubt, by braided uniforms,
gaudy medals, and years of too-rich living.

When our leader visited his capitulating palace
the coifed and perfumed president had said to her
'You may choose to be facetious with my Council, madam,
but I assure you this will not end well for you.'
Well, she smiled, the coup had already finished the bastards off:
their generations of power and wealth meant nothing when
up against the wall or tossed from helicopters into jungle, sea,
or facing whatever form of death entertained exhausted rebels.
The president madly still demanded our surrender
while our captains debated where to hang him.

How will we live after those frenzied days?
Evasively — evading mostly memory
and the remnants of dismembered families.
Putting treachery, lies, deceit, out of mind,
we will move into non contemplative times,
among these groves of mango trees
we've inherited from the recently dead,
and evade recognition of how similar
our lives have become
to those we fought so fervently against.

Full Moon

Above the broken house, a too-large moon
rises over its dozen watchful windows.
A dog plod foots up the hill
on the road where the soldiers came,
the one the old man takes to go fishing,
precarious on his bike with rods and tackle.
The click of a bicycle changing gear
so like soldiers releasing
the safety catches of their guns.
The moon above the broken house
reveals one dog, one fisherman
caught in the crossfire.

King David in Manchester

"I will go unto the altar of God, who gives joy to my youth." —Psalm 42:4.

Clearly the psalmist's youth was never spent
in my grimy Manchester suburb after the war.
True, we did play enjoyable games,
a swarm of post-war kids in the streets,
though even that was undercut
by being bullied to the edge of torture.

It is likely David, King of Judah and Israel,
wrote the psalm about joy in his youth.
It's not our grimy suburbs that are to blame;
David would have been a randy dandy on the razz
among our terraced houses and rough gangs.
His slingshot firing marbles like a machine gun
would have done for the sadistic bullies.
The girls would have thrilled to his rhythmic
body moves as he danced in the streets
after the gas lamps lit up at nightfall.
Bathsheba was no pushover, but the scrubbers
around our way would have gone down on their backs
before his holy charm had thought to ask.

But then the God-intoxicated poet,
his passions overflowing in all directions,
would have been an unlikely fit in our place.
The mean streets, rationed, clouded with coal dust,
were far from Jerusalem, despite the hymns we sang.
'O my son Absalom!' was hardly how we kids
were addressed by our dads back from their war.
And the quiet old men whose sons had not returned
neither danced nor wildly sang their heartbreak to their God;
foreign to Mancunian ways of mourning.

Their Mother Reads Them The Iliad

Catherine and David, beloved of Athene,
attack the serried Trojan lines on the blacktop,
then duck in behind the immortal SUV.
Out to throw their bronze-tipped spears at mighty Hector
and his hardened troops next door. Held for a moment
by bright Apollo's bewitchment of their arms.
Leaves red around them, the last apples on the trees.

"My heroes, another year of this fruitless war!"
shouts Catherine. The picket fence takes a hail of arrows.
Swift-footed next-door kids are felled by Myrmidons
at the shore of the wine-dark pond, thick with heroes' bodies,
their last sight the water lilies, the island-speckled sea,
before Hades' darkness leaks down into their eyes.

Zeus spirits them behind the shed to their own garden,
from where, blind with rage to revenge their fallen comrades,
they throw their arms into fiery combat yet again.
Leeks, lettuce, peas in neat green lines border the battlefield.

Beloved of Athene, Catherine and David have retreated
to the topless-towering cherry tree, alarmed
the Trojans will burn the picnic table and playhouse,
destroying all hope of returning home in time
for tea and cakes with Achilles, breaker of men,
in stately Peleus' high-built kitchen nook.

What's Hecuba to them that they should weep for her?

What We Couldn't See

Sometimes on our way to school
we climbed up and looked over the wall
into the rich man's garden,
through the fruit trees
and across the lawn to the wide terrace,
bright with spring flowers,
to the gray stone house
and the old man himself
sitting reading a paper in the sun,
his children and grandchildren
preparing for their entitled days.

What we couldn't see from there
was the old man's grandfather, after midnight
beside a dark field leading up to woodlands
waving to his Protestant wife and their children
who were being taken by guides
skilled at evading Nazi patrols
along paths through trees to Switzerland,
then on through Portugal to his cousin in England.
Nor see him, again at night, in a basement
wrapping his modest collection of Impressionist canvasses,
and sending them disguised to the same cousin
with the last shipment of shoes from their Hamburg factory.

This man of many wiles, his passport stamped with a red J,
then hid, and ran, and hid, and ran,
finding consolation in visions
of his family at home in England.

My Friend in the Secret Police

I thought if you keep them laughing they can't torture you.
They can, it turned out.
'I am not here to cure you,' I said on his behalf,
'I am just the pain.'

He did laugh a little at that.
I tried to make a further joke on the same theme,
and did credit Herzen,
but his professionalism rather undid me.

'You see, life,' he said, 'is the sum of the functions
by which death is resisted.
Xavier Bichat, I quote in turn,' I think he said.
A noise from somewhere close by made it hard
to hear him, even though he had stopped laughing.
My inadequate jokes, I acknowledged.

'The task is to interfere with as many of those functions . . .'
I apologized later that I had failed
to make out the rest of what he said.

When I could speak again,
I told him that I really didn't know
the answer to the riddle he was posing.

'I know,' he said pleasantly. 'Don't worry. I know.'

23

Myth and History

24

Trebizond

**Some claim that the most memorable first line of any English language novel
of the 20th. century is Rose Macaulay's "'Take my camel dear,' said my aunt
Dot as she climbed down from this animal on her return from High Mass."
[The Towers of Trebizond]**

Mention of Aunt Dot's camel after Mass
brings to mind the Towers of Trebizond
and Xenophon's killing march up country
with his army of ten thousand men
arriving at the hills above the town
shouting 'the sea, the sea!'
And in that sea an island
with a gate of ivory and a gate of horn
where Thetis brought her golden son
before the battles at Troy —
during which, to the silent horror of the gods,
her Achilles, breaker of men, was broken.

Jason had earlier sailed by Trebizond
with his Argonauts, seeing the small town on a green shore
purpled around by the rhododendrons
from whose honey Xenophon and his Ten Thousand
gorged themselves and grew crazed.
Jason returned past the small town
jubilant with his two prizes —
the Golden Fleece and Medea,
the loving woman who had won it for him.

Unlike all other kin-killers
in the stories of the Greeks,
Medea lived a good life in Athens
after her mind-numbing revenge
on her unfaithful husband —
terrifying to gods and humans.
Jason, desolate, suffered through hollow years,
until, lying down to sleep on the beach,
he stretched out under the rotting Argo
hoping to dream no doubt of better times

and was crushed beneath its collapsing stern.
Aunt Dot, less dramatically,
failed to convert the Turkish women
now living in old Trebizond
to the enticements of high Anglicanism,
but the camel failed in nothing.
It carried Dot's niece, camping gear,
Bibles, and other impedimenta
along the Black Sea shore, then south,
uncomplaining if sour-tempered,
through the Levant, setting sail from Jaffa
to England where it made itself, again,
casually and superiorly at home.

Tough Choice

Camels, a star, and princely silks,
the distant shouts of children,
some old man nearby
trying to cough up whatever's
in the cavity behind his ribs,
and Herod calculates —
public opinion, mothers' wailing,
maybe disaffected soldiers —
given the twitch even in the grim eyes
of the Prefect of his palace guards
who'd have to do the job.

Madmen following stars.
How tiny a risk that it might be true,
yet so simple the absolute assurance.

His inscrutable Prefect waited.
Herod looked up at that slab of brutal face
with its disturbing intelligent eyes,
shifted on his throne, calculating.
'Do it,' he could say, and it would be done.
Or, 'Tomorrow let's check Caesarea.
And, Gaius, bring some girls and good wine.'

Odin's Eye for Knowledge

**The tales about the Norse god Odin describe how he gave
one of his eyes in return for seeing all knowledge.**

Tell us, Odin, how could you have done that deal?
Not so much the pain and loss of an eye,
but surely you reflected on
what you'd be getting in return?
For creatures in time, what delight is left
if you know the end with the beginning?

All hope was amputated from your life:
and without hope, could even a god
have enough courage to get through the day?
You knew that Fenris-wolf would be released
and you'd be ground bloody in his great teeth
when Ragnarök was fought and all was lost in fire.

In awe, we still catch glimpses of you on stormy evenings
leading the Wild Hunt of the dead across the winter sky.

But how could you face the mornings
knowing how Balder, your beautiful son, would die?

Horace Odes II.14.

A free, not to say, unhinged, translation of 'Eheu fugaces, Postume.'

Aw, sod it, mate, we've pissed our years away.
Neither pilates nor piety can smooth our wrinkles now,
nor keep us crumblies from the eternal dumpster
unignorably beckoning at the end of the street.

Well, *mon ami,* bit late to give the moral life a try,
after all the parties and cocaine.
Three-hundred days a year of penance at the gym
or incensed meditation, whimpering in the pews,
will hardly sway uncaring Death, who's heard it all.

Royals or working stiffs, or duds like us,
all slopped into the same sluggish sump—
facing this, none of it matters a fig.
Hardly worth the effort, then,
like Sisyphus pushing his bloody rock.

Christ, mate, remember the lovely women
and the Greek island where we had such dazzling times,
the olive trees around our sun-besotted houses—
short-lived and mindless though we were,
they meant a lot to us,
and what do you suppose our absence means to them?

Our only comfort is we'll never know
how all we've loved will now be pissed away.
What lucky bastards will guzzle
the heavenly vintages in my cellar,
which drunks will slop on the mosaics —
and that'll be my legacy,
some wine stains on a floor.

The Ejection of Lewis West, M.A.

The list of rectors and vicars
of St. Michael & All Angels Church,
in what was for some time called Cumberland,
begins with Eustace de Trewik in 1272.
The names of the subsequent holy or unholy men
process down the roll, as down the centuries
they preached, baptized, married, buried
in this green place, among hardy hills,
and in all weathers, ministering
to changing congregations of happy
or unhappy, sane or unhinged souls.

Until 1646, when, an intrusive note tells us, that
Lewis West, M.A. had been 'Ejected'.
For a decade already he'd held the Living.
Doctrinally suspect? Royalist sympathies?
Perhaps a whiff of incense in a Puritan climate,
or could it have been a moral matter?
Though incense, politics, morality in those days
of turbulent religion were intricately tied.

Bracketed together, the next three incumbents —
Lancelot Lowther, John Billingsley, M.A.,
and Daniel Broadley—are noted in the margin as:
"Intruded during the Commonwealth."
No suggestion of approval or disapproval —
you never know who might be reigning next —
nor when the note was added, nor its tone.
While they served their turns, at the Commonwealth's intrusion,
Cromwell had been busy killing people for God,
incensed Catholics with special fervor.
And had been early in the queue to sign
the death warrant for ill-fated King Charles.

Cromwell dead, the monarchy Restored,
and Lewis West M.A. was re-instated,
serving his second term till '68,
when death or age retired him.

He liked a king, it might seem fair to guess,
and couldn't stomach being safeguarded
from sin and error by the pious Lord Protector,
whose Commonwealth we might prefer
to that of Master West.

Pomeranian Summers

The excitement began to build each year
when the leather trunks with satin linings
arrived in carriages from Worth of Paris.
As we tried the dresses on, seamstresses
struggled to make changes while we shouted
giggling accusations about friends' schemes
to hook an innocent von Witzleben
or a von Thadden, or, best hope among
our set, a von und zu Saxe-Altenburg.

The young men received in varnished boxes
matched sets of Krieghoff guns and British Purdeys,
and strutted in the latest hunting gear.
In the afternoons they would hunt *Wildschwein*—
the wild boar that could be relied upon
to run but not to hide, as they themselves
were hunted by sisters' and cousins' friends.

In those Wilhelmine years there were parties every week
and two or three in good and giddy weeks.
Tiaras and jewels glittered and shone,
new gas lights among crystal chandeliers,
a thousand candles on the side tables
among champagne, caviar in glass bowls,
sweet confections in margarita glasses,
and colourful mounded delicacies.

The young women floated in high-waisted dresses,
ruffed sleeves, daring bodices, stiff-pleated lace.
Their suitors in uniforms, silk sashes
and gleaming braid, striped high collars, with medals,
for what, so young, one hardly could imagine.
Laughing they set about the work of courtship,
family fortunes and influence at stake,
while energetic mothers alertly
managed and maneuvered and competed
to expand their families' lands and wealth.

And the afternoon fuss arranging us
for photographs! Bluff mustachioed men
along the rear, shouldering their guns,
the young men and women at the sides
or those of us who could be cajoled to join.
Young children sat compactly in the front.
The dead animals spread across the grass;
in the background, steaming horses and smoking grooms.

For us a magic time before politics,
the Kaiser forever in place, our world
would go on like this, it seemed, forever,
too deep, too steady, too solid to change.
I see us now, looking out from those photos,
blond or dark, smiling or solemn faced,
quite unprepared to be the ones who would
watch the eternal money drain away:
a drip, a steady flow, a stream, a river,
and then the shock, the vast sucking whirlpool.

It started with the sale of a field or two,
for dresses, new hunting rifles, gambling,
property repairs, a son's reckless debts.
A faster drip might mean a village sold.
Each sale was temporary, hardly noted,
to be made better when finances were repaired,
or whatever was supposed to make money
come in again faster than it went out.

The boys were men by the time of the first
great war, which we survived with little loss—
the trenches, after all, were for lesser families
and the scum of towns and farms.
But for some reason costs increased and then
the steady flow became a constant stream,
which required the loss of our beloved villa
by the lake at Wannsee where we'd learned to sail.
Then further debts required our Berlin house.
Fortunately it was no one's favourite,
and needed repairs we could ill afford.

But then the stream became a constant river
that bore away our much-loved Schloss near Königsberg,
where we had hosted our fair share of glittering evenings.

Our young selves in the old photos became
the men and women who were overtaken
and then undone by what was worse than politics.
The family estate came under threat:
unstanchable debts, and vulgar Nazis.
They sent old Prussians, who expressed reluctance
with old-world charm, but those who had sent them
crudely insisted that we should "donate"
our great house and lands to their absurd Reich.

Helped by the Prussians we negotiated
into the war years. But their successors
lacked all charm or interest in discussion,
and one cannot negotiate with victors in arms.
Our new communist comrades' *Bodenreform*
was the whirlpool that sucked our lands under,
and with them our money, and final hopes.

Their land "reform" another word for theft.
The lands of our estate were "reassigned"
and the house was left to nature's lack of care
for what we build and what and whom we love.
This most destructive of all wars destroyed
the family, and those few who survived
followed the contemptible Nazis' rat-runs.
A distant cousin in the north of France
took me in, and I do menial work,
some tutoring, and, still here, I write this.
Those Pomeranian summers are now
gone under history, leaving little mark.
We learned that fortunes come and fortunes go.
Our fortune gave us those summer parties,
and I am perhaps the last who remembers them,
their warmth and smell, the bright excited voices,
the light dresses, the crisp, dark uniforms,
and all our idle lost glittering hopes.

The satin-lined leather trunks, covered in dust,
perhaps in an attic somewhere in Russia,
the hunting rifles fixed on a wall maybe—
the fortunes of war—in Omsk, Dijon, or Texas.

Encounter in a Greek Village

In a coastal village somewhere south,
weathered limestone, bald head to muscled chest,
'assumed', the note beside it said, 'to represent Death'.
The rough eroded face and ill-shaped cavern-eyes
seem to suck all other meaning from the place.

Little visited in its single-room museum:
a few urns, bowls, a cracked sarcophagus,
a female head, noseless but serene.
Next door a bar with folding chairs and two high stools.
Wherever Death had sat before, on temple plinth,
a home or public square, all now gone, repurposed,
and his hunk of stone a shape no one could use,
or was too intimidated to try.

Worn folds of straggled beard, contemptuous lips,
or perhaps the beginning of a smile.
He's not relaxed, looks raw-nerved,
something tentatively polite about him, irresolute.
I can't find a spot to catch him eye to eye:
the small black caverns focus far beyond me.

An owl hoots in the darkening air.
I invite Death for a drink at the bar next door
where we might sit elbow to elbow.
I'll concede we're all headed Lethe-ward anyway,
and his hesitance inviting us across the river,
expecting our reluctance and excuses,
which he'll feel duty-bound to overrule, seems
nothing we can't sort out over a Mythos beer.

The Goddess's Head

The summer wind makes the door clap,
and hissing sand scrapes the windows.
Centuries of winds like this
have carried grit that bites the skin
and wears the fluted columns smooth
and scours the Goddess's one-breasted trunk—
each year less like the perfect body
her sculptor freed from marble
at least two thousand years before.

When the wind has stopped
we will continue searching
along the rocky outcrops by the shore
for her weather-battered head,
lost when she'd tumbled in a storm,
and put her back together as she was
and see if she was frowning or serene.
Roman copy of Greek original,
we'll set her on a firmer plinth
among a few slim cypresses
at the end of a field of olive trees.

Artemis, Hera, or Aphrodite?
The contestants in our idle guesswork.
A more sexualized pose for Aphrodite,
something more maternal, wifely for Hera.
Our statue's coy athletic beauty
and the bunching of her left hand
suggest she once had held a bow,
and so is likely Artemis.

Yet without the head, without the face,
she stays anonymous,
just a worn, though shapely, piece of marble
that might have served for many goddesses
who serve in turn our psychic purposes:
a pattern of love—sacred, maternal, erotic;
friend, lover, enemy to humans,

embodying peacefulness or vengeance;
bringers of fruitful harvests, winter, death;
supporters of culture, arts and crafts,
or in contempt of all human activities.

But we'll re-mount this graceful Artemis
drained of her drama and potency
by centuries of alien gods and
the scouring winds of our skeptical world.

Fly-Bottles

"A philosophical problem has the form: 'I don't know my way about.'" (section 123), and hence the aim of philosophy is "to show the fly the way out of the fly-bottle" (section 309). —Ludwig Wittgenstein, *Philosophical Investigations*.

Freud and Hitler sitting back to back
taking coffee and cake in the Cafe Landtmann,
after their strolls along Vienna's Ringstrasse.
Those same chairs on other days
would have borne the weight of . . .
well, you know the crowd . . . Trotsky, Karl Popper,
Alma Mahler, Klimt, a Wittgenstein or two,
Hayek, Tito, Stalin, Robert Musil, and so on.
A testimony, of some kind, to what
throwing different groups of people together
in freedom, of some kind, can produce.

Behind the Ring, in Vienna's busy bars
invaded by summer flies, the sweating waiters
fixed empty bottles upside down.
The flies' delight in glycerol
led the poor critters, smelling beer,
to find the neck and dive up for
the sweet and damp, to eat and breed.
But found only fumes and darkish emptiness.
They'd spend an hour or more batting their heads
against the bottles' sides until,
exhausted, they fell dead.
The waiters swept them up at end of day.

We too have been seduced, betrayed
by our defective language's sweet promise of
the glycerol of truth.
The buzzing voices of the city falter,
and waiters come with brooms at closing time.

Dead on the Pages

Hunting mushrooms in a Polish forest,
the rusting corner of a metal box
pressed up by roots and rain.
Inside, a waterproofed book;
an unfamiliar orthography,
the text laid out like poetry.

'Ah, the last speakers we know of died
more than a century ago, There are none left'—
the Posnan professor told us — 'who can read this script,
or understand it, if read.
I have others,' pointing to the wall,
seven or eight books on a shelf.
'A Lithuanian colleague thinks his mother heard
the language in the markets as a child.
We have scholars trying to decipher them,
but little hope; there's no Rosetta stone.'

One final glance through the book:
small black slugs who'd died in torment on the page
silently singing their death song, hermetic verses
to no-one who can understand.

Homer Dreaming

**'The blind man who lives on rocky Chios;
his songs are the best, now and forever.'
—Homer's Hymn to Apollo.**

Homer dreaming all those years ago
of Brad Pitt, muscled legs, courtesy of CGI,
powering him up the beach under his Myrmidons' shields,
Achilles toppling the towers of Troy,
a tough cookie with anger issues.
And what would they have done,
who would have heard of Hector,
had not Achilles and his crew turned up?

If your market is for stories of war
then of war and men's anger you must sing,
of how each died from spear thrusts through the face
or under chariot wheels, from arrows tearing organs
of men who fight like wild boars rending hounds
and fall as sheaves of wheat before a band of reapers.
How the gods laughed and wept at humans' plight,
the noise, the bloody gear and sand, the horses
screaming — oh, how we have made horses suffer!—
while cranes croaked indifferently overhead.

But we seek tamer things,
tepid passions, fretful minds, bodies bruised
— at the gym or by cosmetic procedures —
without any god's willful agency:
local transit policy, office enmities,
bodily fluids and adolescent narcissism.

Remote from the sweat of enflamed battle,
from antique zeal about hazards to the soul,
from gods' universal plans, and
the eternal punishments we've merited:
the anger of Achilles not our only dream
soured to a nightmare of inconsequence.

The Tsar's Pullman

Look at this Pullman rail car, silent, still.
Romanov gold with proud black eagle heads,
painted bucolic panels, velvet curtains
with gold tasseled sashes, stained glass windows.
Wrought iron steps climb to an open platform
where the Tsar could be seen by his people,
if duty dragged him from the gorgeous lounge.

Two lounge cars, two diners, and two sleepers,
were built — a bit too late — for the last Tsar
for traveling across his unending,
ending empire. Paid for, delivered, and idle
when crazy war engulfed them all.

After the revolution this lounge car
fetched up here, a gross embarrassment.
Under a galvanized corrugated shed
on this siding of a suburban marshaling yard
on the outskirts of Yekaterinburg,
kept for other uses later, but other
uses never came, and memories died.

Its slow, unmoving journey through harsh time
strips molecules from it every moment.
Ultraviolet light, however dim,
sucks the vigour out of brilliant colours.
The heavy orange velvets sag
under unrelenting gravity.
Surfaces erode, wood fibers crumble,
and varnished woods darken, craze, and crackle.

The rusting wheels have some long way to run
through time, but will not clack along the rails
of Russia's endless snow-packed forests
they were bought for. Nicholas and family
will not look out those windows at his serfs,
who are no longer serfs though serving others.
Maybe found again, spruced up, a tourist attraction

from which the serfs' descendants can look out
at steel and glass, reflecting on time and change.

The History Man

"Thucydides of Athens wrote this history of the war between the Peloponnesians and the Athenians. It begins at the moment that hostilities broke out, as I believed that it would be a great war, more worthy of describing than any that had preceded it." — Thucydides

The austere Thucydides of Athens
inherited a great estate that spread
along the fair river Nestos in Thrace.
Conveniently, it included a gold mine.
He was not short of an obol or two,
and could indulge a quiet passion —
discovering and disclosing the truth —
an uncommon aim and hard affliction.

Some days he rode down to the headland
where the Nestos poured into the sea.
He loosed his horse, sat, observed, and thought.
Despite the vast flow from the river,
why does the sea not rise higher?
And this is one river among hundreds.
'Beyond the horizon it falls into an abyss',
was the commonest answer he received.
When he pointed out there was no evidence for this,
the experts shrugged and said it could be so.

Thucydides rode slowly home.
The stories told about his wartime generalship
were already many and ridiculous,
as were those about all other events
in the war with which he was familiar.

If the wisest cannot solve the puzzles
of rivers and the sea and stars, at least
we can surely discover and disclose
the truth about our own human events?
He determined to give the first true account
so people would forever know what happened
in the great war between Athens and Sparta,

that is destroying the whole Greek world.
He would use his exile and his money
to inquire from those who took part in it
what they had witnessed of what was done
by the strong and suffered by the weak.
He would show that war was a tragic disease;
so when symptoms like these occur again,
people will know what is going to happen next,
and can avoid such all-devouring conflicts.

So he began the first and greatest history book:
"Thucydides of Athens wrote this history."

Seven Oaks Ago

47

A Cloistered Virtue

48

Points of the Compass

Measles, I think it was, ensured I missed
Sister Veronica's classes on Points of the Compass.
I later grasped the idea from her proud mnemonic
as she pointed to the electric light switch
and said to the dimmer of the Dutton twins,
'E is for electricity and east;
east is over there.'
More than seventy years later
I still need a moment to sort east from west,
orienting myself by that now demolished classroom.

As Sister Veronica pointed to the electric east
I noticed mostly the clear pink skin
of her film-star features, gleaming softly with Grace
under the white strip of her wimple.
Her brief frown, moment of impatience,
relaxed into her all-sweet-accord smile,
glittering eyes, divinely perfect teeth.

My sense of east and west
tangled in the confusions
of my first and purest love,
setting all my compasses awry.

The Fall

I felt corruption overwhelm
my pious Catholic childhood.
Remember the name Wilkinson —
Terry the son, Bernard the dad.
They were agents of the devil.
Terry's father famed among us
as a municipal bus conductor.
The day of my sad fall from Grace,
we kids clambered to the top deck
of his bus, our swim trunks wrapped in towels.

Mr. Wilkinson came up the stairs,
strode up the aisle, taking money, giving tickets
and ostentatiously nodding
while pointing at, as though checking off,
those who'd already paid.
The bus fare was tuppence;
I held out both my coppers.
Instead, he pointed and nodded
at each of us kids, falsely counting us
among the ticketed elect.

Then Terry whispered to us all,
'If an Inspector comes to check,
we're to say we just got on
at the last stop'.
He grinned with sheerest joy and pride
at his family's breathtaking deceit.
True, the Wilkinsons were Protestants,
as were most of the kids on the bus —
was it this tbat caused the gross dishonesty?
Even then I doubted it was so simple.

And all the kids exulted as
we got off, tuppences unspent,
now spendable on sweets.
Their delight became mine also,
and I was led to see, oh lord,

how sweet it was!
So I became complicit
in how this world works,
intimate with dazzling knowledge.

The Church Triumphant

Look at these statues of decommissioned saints
from decommissioned churches, lined up
like the warriors of Xi'an
in this Cathedral basement.

A fastidious sergeant-major
or patron saint of meticulous order
has sorted them in ranks, a parade ground
of painted superstars
ready for a celestial party.

Come, amble between rows,
look at this dark square,
twenty or more St. Teresas of Ávila,
black veiled, white wimples around their faces.
Hollywood inspired,
not like the Rubens portrait
capturing her toughness
and intelligence,
and her unsettling ecstatic love of God
embodied in Bernini's carving.
No sense of the political power-dealer,
politicians fawning in her wake.

And look here, across the aisle,
a small, low forest of St. Francises,
a block of more than thirty
brown habits, white knotted cords.
Birds stuck on shoulders,
Disneyesque fawns wide-eyed by knees,
the occasional pacified wolf.
Oddly weak faces
for so hard and gristly a man,
unflinching, welcoming the fiery poker
when an eye needed cauterizing.

And all the other saintly soldiers,
away into the distance.

A small acre of
the Christ himself,
pointing to his burning heart
or arms out to welcome us home,
and a cohort of white and blue Virgins—
both sets irreproachably Aryan.

During silent afternoons
do they discuss what they are waiting for?
Expecting to return
to marble plinths with candles
and kneeling worshippers below them?
Or, saintly, are they resigned,
consoling one another,
their heroic virtues, like their statues,
now redundant?

Latin Class

Father Dunstan entered the classroom
like a bird, think heron,
or crane, long creaking legs
hidden under his Franciscan habit.
He slowly placed the Latin textbook
like a box of pearls, centered precisely
on the table.

'Now, my angelic charges,
I have a secret to impart to you.'
He raised a hand, as though in warning,
and rushed over to the windows,
peering out, pushing one open,
leaning this way and that.
This was routine for our Latin class.

Satisfied, he came back to the table.
'If anyone is wearing a wire,
now's the time to squeal, spill the beans.
If I find out later . . . What was that?!'
Slowly on tip-toe towards the door.
He paused, holding the handle,
ear against the jamb,
then swung the door dramatically wide,
jumped out into the corridor,
looking right and left.
No one snooping today.

'O.K. I don't want it to get beyond
the walls of this room,' a pause,
'or the ceiling and floor, naturally.
Now, internally, swear you will tell no one
what I am about to tell you.'
He gave us a few moments,
then stage-whispered in an awed voice,
'The secret is about some irregular
uses of the pluperfect tense.'

At the end of the class, he swept up his book,
strode to the door, paused again:
'Whatever you do in life, boys,
never underestimate the pluperfect!'
I had maintained, and maintain, my sworn vow
so can't, of course, tell you what we learned that day.

Learning About the Psalms

We called it XD, for Christian Doctrine —
mostly about the ways Catholicism got it right
and all the others wrapped themselves in error.
And dully expecting much the same when
Father Adrian was to teach about the Psalms.

Thin, grey-haired, energetic, self-contained
he slid neatly behind the small table at the front,
and waited a moment till everyone was still.
In his clear, quick, clipped voice he began:
'If you look at any religion in operation
you will find a morality;
when you look at it reflecting on life and itself
you will find a theology;
but, my dear boys,
when you get to the very heart of a religion
you will find a song.
The song at the heart
of Judaism and Christianity
is the psalms.'

It came with the force of revelation.
This elderly, bright-eyed Englishman
connecting hymns and psalms with songs and carnival
displaced years of dreary tuneless droning
with images of King David, ecstatic, singing, dancing,
a naked wild man in the streets of Jerusalem.
Not how we were encouraged to behave
in the churches of my youth.

The image of the dancing psalmist
suddenly seemed like hope.
Though I hadn't realized
how much I needed it.

The Greatest Pleasures

Out into the sun and the cool of autumn on the skin
through the rear door of the Novice House
for our lethal recreation, our rules-light form of football,
in shorts, shirts, and boots, feeling only half familiar
after the Franciscan habit and sandals.
You came out beside me, Father Paul,
taking the shallow steps up to the sandy pitch,
and said, "Bear in mind, Frater, that
the greatest pleasures are intellectual."

You see, Father, more than 60 years on
I have borne it in mind — an odd comment
from a devout and unworldly friar.

With a wife and children, and grandchildren,
and a life of books, I remain as puzzled now as then.

You spoke with such authority and conviction
and even if I was not convinced, it sounded so good
I was happy to carry it with me, to examine
now and then, and drop into conversations,
that maybe puzzled friends as much as you had puzzled me.
Though I've come increasingly to suspect
you were just making a clerical joke.

That cool and sunny autumn day
you played your usual berserker football,
free from the disciplines of everyday friary life—
where the greatest pleasures were spiritual—
you slashed at the ball cheerfully roaring,
taking energetic, exalting part,
as though you thought the greater pleasures physical.

But now, for me, around the dinner table,
sharing a complicit smile with a grandchild—
the greatest pleasures are familial.

In a Friary Cloister

Slap of my sandals, flap of my habit,
rustle of rosary beads
hung over the white cord at my waist,
arms in the capacious sleeves, head down,
walking close to the wall, towards the Sacristy.

On a stone ledge of the central courtyard
a friar was reading, back against a rounded column,
the sun bright on a stack of old books beside him
and on the large one open across his knees.
Father Gerald, a Canon Lawyer — we novices had heard —
here to consult rare books in our library.

He smiled up as I approached,
pointed to the ledge beyond his books,
inviting me to sit opposite him
within the cloister arch.

'Have you noted, frater,
how hard it is to build something well,
and how easily it is destroyed?'
This was not the kind of conversation
I had been made familiar with.
'I had learned this as a general principle, father,
though it has not much impinged on my experience.'

He nodded, smiled again, looked
at the shrubbery in the cloister's courtyard,
then at the big book open on his knees.
'You have lived in fortunate times, frater.
I mustn't keep you from your duties.'
I rose, walked onward to the Sacristy
and have felt ever since
that I gave him the wrong answer

New Gods of Instagram & Twitter

Superannuated gods,
old and wrinkled gods,
hollow-eyed gods,
more dust than echo from their beaten ribs.
'Kindly form a queue to the left.
You have my deep sympathy, all,
and please have your forms filled out.'

I am springingly young
and thumpingly strong;
watch my muscles ripple to music;
feel that forested thigh —
careful now, madam.

My astonishing versatility, ladies and gentlemen,
has attracted two further responsibilities:
what to do with old confessional boxes,
and, oh dear, what to do with redundant gods.

The old confessionals,
often carved by masters,
I'll purvey to kinky hotels
as clothes closets, wardrobes.
Just think, madam, of the frisson
draping your daring gowns
in these dark-wood armoires —
in which what sins were confessed! —
with shelving for madam's
fripperies and undies,
whatzits and whatevers,
or sir's liquor cabinet in the games room,
or for guns, if killing is sir's game.

But it's the old gods that vex me.
Some of them galactically enormous,
hands open, apologetic shrugs, rueful smiles,
quite out of miracles and deepest truths,
no smarter than the *New Yorker* or the *TLS*.

And some — you'll be expecting this —
are still as holy as boiling water;
they'll intimidate you out of your skull,
though they're increasingly transparent
and seriously decomposing.

The old days — Creations, Edenic gardens,
tricky tests for mortals, damnation, salvation —
all gone, and now you want some fun — I hear you —
I can see you don't, like, care
about these profitless and prophetless Divinities.
So, let me just get the skids under them.

I know — you're not listening — I'll get used to it —
you're downtown, back against a dumpster, fucking
while I'm trying to raise, or lower, the tone around here —
but keep in front of mind that the god of irony's guns
point in all directions.

'No pushing in line, please,
we'll deal with you one by one,
in the order of your, shall we say, waning.
We'll treat you better than you ever treated us.'
With them out to grass, it'll all be ours —
Paradise, I promise you.

Life and Loves

The Tenure Committee

— What do you consider your most notable contributions?
— My golden sons and radiant daughter. Though
          I must acknowledge
          they were jointly authored.

— Do you have these contributions to hand for our evaluation?
— I seem to have misplaced each one of them,
          at airports, I recall,
          and coming home alone.

— What will be the focus of your future research?
— Studies that fill voids of the kind
          they left when smiling
          they said goodbye.

— Do you have evidence of continuing productivity?
— Inadvertently a number of grandchildren
          for whom I serve as
          a significant endnote.

— And what will be your strategy for future publication?
— My expectation is that I will continue to place articles
          like a squirrel digging moss
          for nut-sized stones.

Declining Accomplishments

He had read Schopenhauer
till the books were ragged,
and his own was added to them —
next on his lacquered shelf
to his earlier books
on Plato's conception of Justice
and Thucydides' sense of Tragedy.

Later he liaised on behalf of his country
with trade delegations
from China and Germany,
and exercised his legal skills
in the highest courts of the land,
and in negotiating tax concessions
from shark-like hi-tech companies.

But in none of these activities
did he experience the high seriousness
and sense of successful achievement
as when negotiating who would draw
the day's road systems on the pavement
and determine the rules whereby
the dinky cars, trucks, and buses would operate
and whose would have what degrees of priority —
they had to consider also whose houses
they would be playing in front of that day,
who had remembered to bring chalk,
the age, quality, and number of dinkies each contributed,
and, not least, relative skills at drawing
branching roadways, bus stops, and the rest.
Peace, order, and happiness depended
on getting that work done well.

Author Addresses Muse

Come out, you cow! I know you're in there,
whimpering in your stinking cave.
I've tried flattery, which gets me nowhere,
tried winkling you out with a wet ear-poke —
metaphorically speaking. Shouted out
some of your past winning lines.

Grunt, Muse! Groan, shriek, stammer!
Anything but whimper like that —
there's no bloody market for it.
I need a starter, a bit of kindling!
I try shouting, 'Sing, Muse,'
— there's nothing but silence,
as though you'd left the building.
Tried "rosy-fingered" or "wine-dark,"
but it's like kicking a motorbike
that's out of fuel.

Exasperated —
against all that's holy —
I rush the cave entrance,
force myself past the briars and boulders,
scour its passages and chambers.
Of course, you aren't there.
Of course, no sign of habitation, ever.
Of course, the whimpering is mine.

Authenticities

There's always someone more authentic than you
who played muddier rugby and broke more important bones
on colder Saturdays
and whose motor-bike had hundreds more ccs;
ready to seize the future as though he had title deed
to its sunlit fields and palaces.
There's that less authentic person scowling at you
from the mirror,
snarling at the future,
"You think I have nowhere else to go?"

There's always someone less authentic than you
who cheated at cards and smirked while acting tough
at office parties
and who was too eager to be thought well of;
failing to see his ploys for self-advancement
absurdly evident to all.
There's that more authentic person
frowning at you from the mirror,
grimacing at the past,
"You think I had somewhere better to go?"

There's always someone about as authentic as you
whose swagger was self-conscious
and relationships were fragile and sometimes broke
and who patched things up and staggered forward,
partly recognizing his need of others
to forgive and keep him going.
There's that unreliably authentic person
watching you from the mirror
shrugging at an ambiguous present,
"You think that's the way to get through this?"

Moving Away

after C. P. Cavafy

You are leaving our city,
and preparing to live in another.
You will miss the mountains,
but your new place also has
a fine river passing through it
reflecting glass and steel towers
in which familiar business is done,
chats with new friends in coffee bars,
and after-lunch strolls by the water.

Each day you will miss us a little less.
We will remark how the loss of you
diminishes our city,
and you will no doubt see how your new life
enhances your new place.

All's set fair; you go with courage and hope,
and you will walk smiling
through your welcoming city's streets.
But you cannot see from there
the wreckage you leave in my heart.

Too Late?

Mrs. Reardon walks down the pavement
which is more broken now than when
she pushed four different children in their prams,
two of whom will be at the funeral today
of the man she married
because the man she loved married her best friend.
Her friend died last year and the man she loved
will also be at the funeral of the man she married.

Mrs. Reardon and the man she still loved
passed on this street with their children in prams,
then he with a son and football
and she with ballet shoes and a daughter,
and with further sons and daughters stopping,
chatting with energetic gaiety.
And the many times they met in supermarket or bookstore
discussing anything intently together for far too long.

Would he, after the funeral, after due time . . . ?
Or will the reserve they had cultivated like a shell . . . ?
Oh, and his once hair . . . her once taut skin . . .

Young Women on the Morning Bus

They have risen early, before the sun,
and sit here gleaming in the bus's lights,
hair like wheat, falling straight to shoulders,
or clipped and coiffed or fashionably frizzed;
their faces moistened, foundationed, powdered,
mascara'd, eye-linered, shadowed, lip-glossed:
products of the morning's skillful labour.
Like princesses of old, too beautiful
for anything except to be admired,
too fraily perfect for a dreary office.

Stylishly, confidently clothed;
scarves of coloured silks and lightest cashmeres
tucked around smooth necks that knights of old
would have braved dragons to kiss.

And the men?
Ach, it makes no sense.

Page Marker

Joe in Dublin driving alarmingly,
glasses clouded with dandruff and dust,
windscreen smeared with pollen, mud, and bird lime.

His wife had brought me here to give a talk
about something. The good lady, sitting,
Irishly, behind the gossiping men, said
'Give him a copy of your new book, Joe.'

He started feeling jacket pockets,
driving one-handed and dim-eyed.

With Canadian courtesy, and fear,
I quickly said I'd be more than happy
to find one in Hodges Figgis bookstore.

'No, no,' he pulled a copy from a pocket,
'I've used this one before for readings,'
shaking it, sprinkling to the floor by his feet
notes, bus tickets, cards, torn bits of paper
he'd used as convenient page-markers,
then handed me the emptied book.

Home in Canada I turned the pages
and saw his shaking had failed to dislodge
a ticket, a business card, a folded note.
Having only the wife's work address
I posted them to her to give to Joe.

When I was next in Dublin, in a pub
he told the sad story of his divorce.
He'd no idea where his wife had found
that letter from his mistress.

Morning by the Sea, with Company

**Apologies for echoes from Tomas Tranströmer's
"Memories watch me." John F. Deane's translation.**

She wore a crisp green jacket —
        or blue, red, orange, whatever colour you want;
        or make it a blouse; you are, after all inescapably
        co-creator of this wreck —
walking by the sea —
        or, well, wherever you want, on the street,
        in the mountains, in fact you don't have to have her walking,
        and I suppose 'she' could be 'he' or 'they' if you prefer—
she had woken early —
        you could perhaps add, somewhat redundantly
        given that she was out by the sea,
        or wherever you decide to put her,
        that it was too late to go back to sleep —
and was crammed with memories —
        well you don't want her vacant or just looking at the waves,
        though I suppose you could have something focus her
        on a specific memory, a stone or shell is usual by seas —
which are jumbled, dissolving as she tries to focus —
        you could instead insist on some specific memory
        and let it suggest further incidents,
        her Madeleine, if you want a classy echo —
        any reference to Proust is classy, don't you think? —
yet somehow close to her, breathing by her ear —
        yes, well I know that's not very straightforward,
        maybe a bit creepy;
        sure, how can memories not be close to you?
        but it seemed evocative; if it doesn't do it for you,
        put in your own image of how she is getting on out there —
scattered by the grating roar of pebbles which the waves draw back —
        ok, the 'classy' reference
        made me think of Arnold's Dover Beach,
        and you might prefer we had earlier agreed
        it would be a pebble beach,
        but you can change that, if you wish,
        I mean, hissing on the sand, or something —

memories of past seas and retreating, dissolving lines behind boats —
        as you say, a bit clichéd,
        but I suppose the sea images took over,
        which you can remove, of course —
among a whirl of seabirds —
        yes, that's the end, not very dramatic, I'll grant you,
        but you could give it a more plangent ending,
        and next time write your own poem; eh, Tomas?

Abrasax

I'm up for the scramble for planets and moons
with Elon, Jeff and the other tech-lords.

I've planned better and am not crazy enough
to fall in with their wacko ambitions
to land on pockmarked chunks of sterile rock,
where lack of gravity, and so much else,
see organs, bones, and muscles wrecked in months.

What kind of life can be imagined there
compared to mother Earth's enfolding warmth,
where we have co-evolved with all this stuff?

I'll be ahead of their absurd ambitions
to make Earth's moon, or Mars, or gloomy Ceres
worth visiting more than once, to hop around;
lethal to attempts at colonizing:
everything, impossibly, has to work
perfectly always; and the crap weather!

My Abrasax rocket, propelled spaceward
by massive Improbability Drives,
has delivered me to a neat planet,
discovered by newly interpreting
the Babylonian star catalogues,
the Elamite tablet of Ammisaduqa,
and hitherto misunderstood calculations
of the sublime Chaldean Saros cycle.
Though landing is tricky and the place damp —
a vast ocean with one patch of dry land,
an equatorial island the size of Ireland —
the planet Abrasax welcomes us home.

On this gleaming Kassite horse of the sun,
this archon of the spheres of Ouranos,
this utopian dream of Basilides,
a second Eden will soon develop:
the sweet warm rain falls in sunshine,

fields packed tight with wheat and barley,
the island fringed with silver beaches
and gray cliffs falling to the ocean,
rich in clamorous sea-birds,
low-rise towns in green valleys
where young and old, at dusk, walk by the rivers.

Kite and Boy

The kite, tail twisting in the wind,
string bellying out, looks down
on the sea's edge far below,
at the boy holding it.

The kite tugs furiously, straining,
singing to the wind for help,
till it lifts the boy.

Knit together
they fly over the trees beside the shore,
over the town, toward the hills.

They swing around each other as they rise.
Which is the planet, which the moon?

As the boy lets the string run out
he feels the tethered kite's
fantasy of freedom.
Then slowly, turn by turn,
he reels it in.

Fighting against the tightening constraint,
it bucks among the squalls above the trees,
swinging in wild arcs,
coming ever closer.

Boy and kite whistle in the wind.

The Cabin in Spring

You said you'd visit in the spring,
so I have prepared since January.

I coaxed the trees to bud, then leaf;
the cherries and the apples
I sang into bunching blossom;
the birds I trained to fly in circles
and as they loop around your head
to call your name.

Thinking you might come across the lake
I painted the boat with light
and rigged a yellow sail.
I fed the fish while playing my guitar
so they would rise in welcome
when I took you on the water.

Then the flowers returned
and the sun invited me to clean the windows,
to add crisp curtains, new duvet,
to polish boards, gleam the stove, while ear-like
speakers overflowed the cabin
rehearsing for your arrival
Pastoral symphony and Spring sonata.

'No, no — no problem. My misunderstanding.'

With lake and birds, fish, trees and rain,
who could ask for more?
I'm patient in the disciplines of love.
I'll eat the flowers.

An Old White European Guy

Satnaving through the suburbs of another Asian town,
skyscrapers as far as he can see, new streets
overnight stuck into the expanding grid,
every added inch swarmed instantly by mopeds.

Miles of scruffy shops, anything you want, or don't,
garages fixing cars, trucks, airplanes, anything,
the rivet guns, the resisting sheer of steel,
loud metallic farting as wheel nuts slam in place,
honking horns, pollution's gritty taste, the human buzz
against the whining continuo of engines.
The boys fixing computers, writing code,
building or dismantling bikes, buses, trains, ships;
the girls in nail-bars, hi-tech assembly,
or power-suited, precariously-heeled,
more confident than God and twice as rich,
running businesses he can't imagine.

Just another exploding Asian town:
the suburbs eat fields, level hills, swallow lakes,
consume ten miles in all directions every day,
90% of the population under five,
and grows ten million every hour,
the noises never stop, the dynamo shrieks on.

Lunging again through the same or different suburbs,
dazed, dazzled, hammered, he's ejected to the airport,
then up from this voracious monster's energy,
on to the next town, before they all merge into one.

Pamela's Birthday

Battered by sun I entered through the Jaffa Gate
into shouting crowds of tour guides and their charges,
into dust, cars, money-changers, stone-paved streets
with well-armed police, better armed soldiers,
and persistent men who promised, threatened,
tours, food, or, if I wished, various depravities.

Anywhere to sit was covered by tourists
whose shouts and laughter bounced off
the walls of King David's Tower.
Moving towards less noise, I saw
an entrance to greenery,
a courtyard of some kind.

No-one stopped me as I ambled in
to sudden silence, shrubs, trees, even bird song.
An Anglican church and guesthouse.
An outdoor restaurant, closed and empty,
opposite the church from which, dimly,
I heard an organ and gently hymning voices.

I sat on a white wicker chair, remembering
a temple near Kyoto,
in whose garden I had wandered
hearing the chanting of priests,
and then a gong through the evening trees
calling to prayer or perhaps a meal.

But then the Englishwomen came,
in flowered dresses, one by one,
intervals of some minutes between each.
They emerged from the guesthouse ahead,
smiled vaguely as they passed,
entering the restaurant's kitchen.

One carried back an enormous cake,
grinning complicitly
as though I must know whom it was for.

Later one asked if she could help me.
I said I was just waiting,
which seemed a right answer,
as she smiled and said 'Ah, good, good.'

Wisteria rose up the posts that held the roof
and spread enthusiastically across it.
I smiled in response to the smile of another
cotton-dressed Englishwoman;
this one slim, blond, and bouncy, with large teeth,
carrying a wide glass bowl of trifle,
heavy with multicolored fruits.

'Looks wonderful,' I said.
'It's Pamela's birthday,' she smiled,
as though anyone who looked so comfortably
at home here must also love Pamela.

Each of the women who walked by
seemed so simply nice
that I was sure I'd love Pamela too.
I said I hoped the party would go well.
'Will you be coming?' she queried almost flirtatiously.
I paused too long, too little: 'I'm afraid I can't make it.'
I have wondered since if saying 'Yes'
would have made all the difference?

Reluctantly I strolled out into the baking streets,
down into the souks, passing
from a brief vision of the Garden of Eden
to its restless, noisy, grim-faced replacement:
one of my life's answers to nobody's question.

Old Lightning

Rain or shine we saw him daily
set out for his morning walk,
taking the steps of the house next door
with high-kneed caution,
steadying hand on the rail,
like someone who has fallen once
and plans not to do so again.
His pace was precise, unhurried,
so we called him Old Lightning.
For fifty years a bee-keeper
somewhere on the fragrant Prairies.
Maybe his work had led him to
his patent gleaming cleanliness,
and given him that gentle face,
yet authoritative—as if
he were an old ascetic monk.
Dressed for his walks in shirt and tie,
his Sunday-church-going clothes.
Of wife, children, friends, we knew nothing.
I saw him walking in the park
one cold dark day, yet he seemed
cocooned in a celestial glow
and the murmur of friendly bees.

81

Trees, Birds, Fish, and Things

Seven Oaks Ago

Why would the branches whisper to me of Caesar?
These coastal woods not those through which he rode.
But, locals say, in the shelter of this hill
trees from acorns from trees from acorns from trees
can span a thousand years. So maybe, seven oaks ago,
he sat under wind-articulating branches
like these that whisper to me here today.

Seated in a tent with his general, Quintus —
some wine, some strategy—two impulsive men,
both with disaster in their eyes, but now just
laughing at the risks of this brash expedition.
Later both wrote to Cicero, Quintus's brother,
letters that marched along the Roman roads,
writing Britain into Europe for the first time.

With legions, horses, baggage, he's long gone
over sea and mountains and the Rubicon.
The kings he left behind were then in fee to Rome.
As I listen to the branches, I hold in my pocket
a silver denarius from a field in Kent
which someone lost here seven oaks ago.

Trees Against Evening Light

It was years ago now,
on a slow bus late in the day,
weaving through villages
south to Oxford.
Heavy cloud above us
but a diffuse and widening strip
of light where the sun was setting,

Tightly woven hedgerows edging fields
with random trees among them.
Then I noticed, sharply etched
against the background glow, a tree's
lace-like starkly perfect shape.
Then a wide-spread weeping willow
gracefully cascading down
the radiant strip of sky.

Gaping at backlit trees, I was pleased
that the unhurried bus
groaned up and down the hills,
halted by traffic here and there,
waited and crawled around roadworks,
paused to drop off women,
impeded by shopping bags,
and schoolchildren, scruffy in their uniforms,
and shuffling pensioners.

Surely I had seen such trees a hundred times,
but now scarce breathing, gazing at
the complex beauty
of a hawthorn's skeleton passing by:
an old and sturdy trunk, heavy branches
slimming towards their tips
stretching out in all directions toward the light.
Oak and beech, an ash exuberantly spread,
a lushly wild-limbed chestnut, a writhing yew,
an elm bushing gracefully in the direction
prevailing winds have pointed.

As the light dimmed
the backlit silhouettes
merged into the darkening sky;
only my face now framed in the window glass.

The Bluffs on Galiano Island

As we sway and turn
in a remote arm of this galaxy,
our dead gray moon
is a tethered drag
on our blue earth.

During a late afternoon like today
you can look through the dark trees
at an immense weight of water
being dragged swirling below,
carrying fish
which seals harvest,
hauling them half-eaten
onto the rocks,
and what we know of this
is the fish smell
that curls and lingers around the cemetery
here on the bluffs.

It will fade in the morning
when fresh tides clean the seals' tables —
our bright galaxy is insensible
to what it carries and drags on our journey.

A Wounded Goose

A ragged V
            of calling geese
                        approaches,
                                    one powering
                                                to take its turn
                                                            at point
                                    as others find
                        their places in
                  the slipstream. Then
            as they rise toward
      the line of trees
                                                one
                                                flailing
                                                body
                                                tumbles
                                                to the
                                                ground;
                  a cry and crash no more than twenty feet away.

It flaps a damaged wing and starts to run
south in the direction of its fellows,
neck straining toward them, stopping at the wall.
The wounded goose and I stand helpless at
this sudden fathomless tragedy.
Well to the south, the wedge climbs onward,
powerful chests heaving tireless wings;
their distant honking to each other fades
as the line dissolves in the evening sky.

How the Sweet Birds Sing

Unlike an English churchyard after dawn,
this western edge of Canada in winter
does not delight us with the sounds of bird song.
Some tweet and chirrup in our raw constraining cold,
but more from reluctant duty it feels,
than any hint of ecstasy.

Beside our house one lonely bird
repeats its two-note call,
holding the first long note,
dropping half an octave for the second,
forlorn, and held just half as long.
It launches this tedious challenge
to any hostile trespasser,
or maybe a cautiously optimistic
come-on to some prospective mate.

And no potential mate could doubt
that a bird able to repeat
all the cold morning
his endless tuneless dirge
must be formidable.

Weeks later he's still at it,
but now just the first note,
which falls off quickly at the end —
too weary to keep up the full aggression or
disappointed in love so early in the year?

Near that English churchyard after dawn,
by the pond where they drowned unwanted kittens,
I first heard a nightingale, or maybe, so early, a lark;
the ecstasy was mine, though I thought it was the bird's.

We cannot read a bird's heart from its song.

Uncertain Signs

I wake from reading a signpost at the crossroads,
crowded round this time of year with bird song
and Queen Anne's lace high as the hedgerow.
I had walked a winding path from the village
through a bluebell wood and from a humped bridge
watched the slow weeds sway with the water.

The place is nowhere,
yet built from where I've been or seen,
paths and streams I've known,
and one May day those shining mounds
of Queen Anne's lace in a country lane.

And I am now so far and long away
I can only conclude
the maker of dreams is out to break my heart.

May Again

Every season has its threats and panics.
Unprepared for, May unsettles us again
with its ready-or-not foretaste of what's to come.

Unstoppable May's planned assault
launches massed stockpiles from underground
assailing us with thuggish greenery.

Ostentatious May comes like a madman
slapping clumps of colour everywhere,
blurs trees and shrubberies with flowers and leaves.

Impulsive May, oiling the spring,
throws petals, seeds, pollen all over us,
menacing us with threats of more.

Profligate May gushes new lambs, new birds,
new-minted beetles, endless things that fly
and bite, along with illusions of hope.

Symbiosis

I don't know what it's like for rats on nights like this;
thunder crackling from the snarling tops of trees,
and November's freezing rain slashing without mercy.
Alertly picking its way across the gravel,
rat slinks behind the shrubs then scampers towards the shed.
Pausing to piss, it sniffs to sense that all is well
before slithering in and down into the fug
of perhaps contented fellowship, snuggling in.
Maybe tumbling amongst tough competitors
or reluctant mates. A mess of charged hostility
which hisses sharp across their sleek and smelly backs.
Much as it might feel for us, coming from rain
to choir practice, board room, or yoga group.

We creatures have been long entwined, rat and human,
sharing our homes and food,
sharing our fleas and flies and filth.
A traveler from some distant galaxy
looking at life on Earth would hardly distinguish
between us: eyes in heads; backbone; hair; tongue; teeth,
that familiar spectrum of emotions—
genetically we're almost identical.

Like cruel siblings we have long engaged in battle
to slaughter one another to extinction.
We humans have been more deliberate killers,
recruiting cats and dogs as allies, and lethal poisons.
Yet your destruction has often been the deadlier —
whole villages extinguished. One third of Europe.
But you found with us gone life was harder.
And if we are successful in your extermination,
we too may be bewildered at the cost we have to pay.

There is no appetite among humans for reconciliation,
so we are in this battle till the end, I fear.
Perhaps I should know better what it's like for rats
on nights like this.

Bird Songs

Three old men outside
around a pub table,
men who were boys together
in this quiet village,
then went their varied ways,
now sit chatting over their pints,
hearing the weir again
and the wind through the leaves
of trees that were half the size
when they were boys.

Tom says, "Even when I see
the wren's beak strain
and its throat throb,
I hear only a few low squeaks
and the rest is inaudible.
It took a while to recognize
the loss was in my ears."
Dick adds, "I hear skylarks
on the south downs behind our house,
high soloists with sudden silent gaps."
Harry nods, "I thought at first
the finches were losing
parts of their song
to environmental damage;
it was like listening to an orchestra
with missing instruments.
I used to whistle, copying birds
with skill enough to get their attention,
but no longer—reedy, breathy,
lips inelastic, my trills all gone."

Even so, happy enough
to be together again by the weir;
losing high frequencies, they knew,
wouldn't be the worst or last of it.

After Many an Autumn

I have seen more than eighty of them
so why should I marvel at another autumn?
However bright, the colours fade,
leaves' lace skeletons shrivel into mould.
The sun has a cataract of high cloud,
and the Ice Queen's sharp kisses and her
shocking embrace overflow old eyes,
the world wobbles and breaks
as I dab at them with Kleenex.

Maybe you think I marvel
because this might be my last?
where you can be casual and profligate.

No, it was none of that:
I marvel at this year's colours,
made in a wet spring, long sunny summer,
then sharp cold.

Stuttering through neighbouring streets
or through the forest is an ecstasy
of what autumn trees can manage
if they really try,

I'm grateful it got the whole thing right
before I go.

94

www.ingramcontent.com/pod-product-compliance
Lightning Source LLC
Chambersburg PA
CBHW070411200726
48294CB00003B/1165